"You don't see rainbows
when you're looking down."
Abbie Jane: Age 12.

ISBN: 978-1-913339-63-0
Text copyright © Claire Thompson 2025
Text copyright © Abbie Jane 2025
Illustrations copyright © Eliott Bulpett 2025
The moral rights of the authors and illustrator have been asserted.

A catalogue record of this book is available from the British Library.
No part of this publication may be reproduced, stored in a
retrieval system or transmitted in any form or by any means
without prior permission from the author. All rights reserved.

ABBIE'S TRUE COLOURS

Written by
Claire Thompson & Abbie Jane

Illustrated by
Eliott Bulpett

First published in the UK
2025 by Owlet Press
www.owletpress.com

Abbie lived in a small town, far away from everywhere, and everything.
Every day was the same, and everyone liked it that way.

Everyone, except Abbie that is.

She felt different.

But the kids at school didn't like different.

So Abbie spent most days looking down at her feet. She made her way home through the thundering rain, swirling her soggy sneakers in the puddles.

"**Abbie, look up!**" Mum called as the rain started to clear.

The rainbow was beautiful.

"You don't see rainbows when you're looking down,"
Abbie said with a hopeful smile.

She wished that she could carry
the colours with her, everywhere.

But that would be impossible.

Unless . . .

She reached into her rainy-day box . . .

. . . and carefully threaded bright beads onto her shoelaces.

Making two tiny rainbows for her feet.

The colours made her really happy.

'Maybe if everyone had a rainbow of their own,
it might remind them to look up, too,' Abbie thought.

So she laced the rainbow onto her shoes, ready for school the next day . . .

But everything was still the same.
Some kids stared and whispered, as usual,
while others didn't notice the beads.

So, as usual, Abbie
stared back down
at her feet.

And yet, something felt different.

Now, Abbie had her rainbow – she could see her true colours.

And Abbie didn't worry so much about feeling different.

She felt braver.

And soon, people did start to notice Abbie's beads.

The bus driver gave her a friendly nod.

Mrs Robins smiled when she saw them.

Some stares turned into curious glances.

"I'd like to wear some beads, too."
Abbie's friend, Max whispered.

So, that night, Abbie made a few more rainbows.

The next morning, Abbie felt more confident.

She pinned up packets of beads for other people to take.

They quickly disappeared. Abbie worried that kids had torn them down.

Her heart sank, but her rainbow beads reminded her to look up . . .

And as she did, Abbie couldn't believe her eyes...

Shoe by shoe, tiny rainbows started popping up all over school.

In English class, Mrs Robins was wearing rainbow beads!

"Abbie, can you tell the class what these beads mean?" she asked.

Abbie looked at her beads and then held her head high.

"I wear rainbow beads on my shoes to show kindness and love to everyone. I wear them because I'm proud of who I am," she said.

And soon, tiny rainbows began appearing all over town.

In the grocery store, the doctor's surgery and even the local police station!

People shared photos. Abbie worried as the postman arrived with piles of letters, but they were from people around the world, all asking for beads!

It was a lot of work making so many packets, but Abbie's family and new friends helped.

One afternoon, Abbie arrived home from school
to find Mum's van was piled high with boxes, bags, and beads.

Abbie's heart raced. She wasn't sure what was going on.

"You don't see rainbows when you're looking down," Mum reminded her.

"Jump in!"

In the city, Abbie gazed at the dazzling parade. Everyone was shining in their true colours.

"**They're all different like me,**" Abbie smiled, handing out beads.

"**No, Abbie...**" Mum replied, her face beaming with pride.

"... they are all BRAVE, just like you!"

And from that day on, Abbie's world was always filled with rainbows.

Dear Reader,

I hope this story helps you see that no matter what people believe in, they deserve support and kindness.

My advice to you is to always show more kindness than what's expected.

Make sure you never change just to fit in.
And, no matter who you are, if one person believes – we can all make a difference.

Being different won't always be easy.

This, my friend, is why it is so important to show your support for others.
Make sure you do whatever is possible to help others.
And always stay true to what you believe in.

Now in case no one has told you,
I am proud of you.

Being different makes you who you are.
And who you are is awesome.

Yours truly, Abs xx

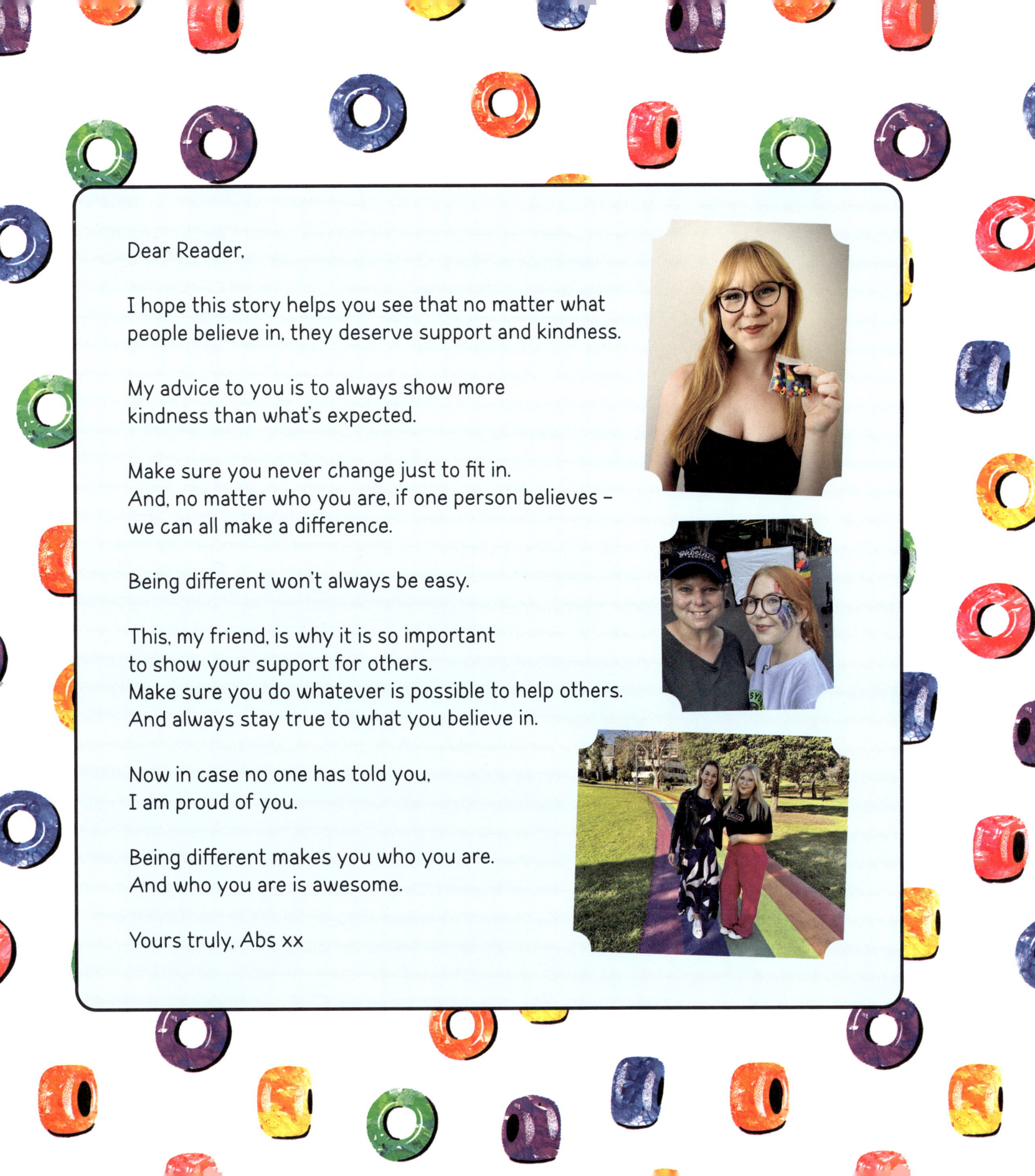

rainbowshoelace.com.au